Barrio Adentro and Other Social Missions in the Bolivarian Revolution

Germán Sánchez

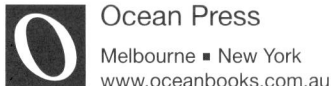

Ocean Press
Melbourne ▪ New York
www.oceanbooks.com.au

Cover design ::maybe

Copyright © 2005 Ocean Press
Copyright © 2005 Germán Sánchez

All rights reserved. No part of this publication may be reproduced, stored in a retrieval system or transmitted in any form or by any means, electronic, mechanical, photocopying, recording or otherwise, without the prior permission of the publisher.

ISBN 10: 1-920888-40-3
ISBN 13: 978-1-920888-40-4

First Printed 2005

PUBLISHED BY OCEAN PRESS
Australia: GPO Box 3279, Melbourne, Victoria 3001, Australia
 Fax: (61-3) 9329 5040 Tel: (61-3) 9326 4280
 E-mail: info@oceanbooks.com.au

USA: PO Box 1186, Old Chelsea Stn., New York,
 NY10113-1186, USA
 Tel: (1-212) 260 3690

OCEAN PRESS TRADE DISTRIBUTORS
United States and Canada: **Consortium Book Sales and Distribution**
 Tel: 1-800-283-3572 www.cbsd.com

Australia and New Zealand: **Palgrave Macmillan**
 E-mail: customer.service@macmillan.com.au

UK and Europe: **Pluto Books**
 E-mail: pluto@plutobooks.com

Cuba and Latin America: **Ocean Press**
 E-mail: oceanhav@enet.cu

www.oceanbooks.com.au
info@oceanbooks.com.au

editor's note

This pamphlet contains a chapter from the book *Cuba and Venezuela* by Germán Sánchez, which is forthcoming from Ocean Press in early 2006. Another pamphlet taken from the same forthcoming book is *The Cuban Revolution and Venezuela*. Germán Sánchez is a Cuban academic and diplomat and has been the Cuban ambassador to Venezuela since 1994.

The themes of this pamphlet are undoubtedly relevant; its tone is informative and reflective. It has been published in light of the importance of making information on Venezuela available to a wide international audience: the alternative vision to neoliberalism it offers, the daily realities lived by both the Venezuelan and Cuban people, and the links that unite both nations.

We hope this pamphlet will be useful and that readers will engage with, argue with, and even criticize its content; that they will begin the adventure of exploring the extraordinary political, social, and historical times which are unfolding for Latin America and for a Venezuela led by Hugo Chávez.

A partial list of Ocean Press books and pamphlets on Cuba, Venezuela, and Latin America can be found at the back of this pamphlet. A full list of titles—in both English and Spanish—can be found at **www.oceanbooks.com.au**

Barrio Adentro and Other Social Missions in the Bolivarian Revolution

INTRODUCTION

On December 31, 2002, I had a brief conversation with President Hugo Chávez in his office at Miraflores Palace. Just a few minutes before saying good-bye, with both of us still seated, he stated with customary eloquence and complete confidence: "We have concluded an extremely difficult, dangerous year, during which we had the initiative on very few occasions. But, despite almost always hitting back from against the ropes, we won the battle. Today we have concluded this defensive phase. From tomorrow, we will initiate the new, offensive stage of the revolution."

Hugo Chávez's assertion was without nuance. More than listening to his words I observed his firm gestures and expression, and noted his serene conviction, although it was clear he did not have a plan of action in mind to make that assertion a reality. I farewelled the president convinced he would know how to lead his people and further triumph in the face of new threats. The lessons and the formidable victories against the fascist coup plot of April and the December oil strike were behind him. The year 2003 promised to be equally complex and decisive for the Bolivarian process. Securing immediate benefits for the people and completing the political defeat of the opposition and its foreign allies were urgent tasks.

In January 2003 the president and Venezuelan government were forced to devote their full attention to defeating the oil strike. By February, offensive measures were beginning to be more evident: exchange controls were established putting an end to the multimillion-dollar flight of capital of recent weeks. That decision became an effective and opportune antidote to the collapse of the economy, which had suffered the ravages of destabilization.

Without any doubt, from September 2001, US President Bush's policy toward Venezuela toughened—short-term US policy was to remove Chávez from power. The aggressive actions of the bloc of the Venezuelan bourgeoisie and oligarchy and the Bush administration largely prevented the Bolivarian government from implementing its social and economic programs intended to benefit the people. Nevertheless, a large proportion of poor people—more than 65 percent of the population—maintained their faith in Chávez, and his promises, and continued to trust in the strength of the Bolivarian constitution, which had been approved in the referendum of December 15, 1999.

But how long could those poor people, greatly affected by the crisis, wait for a new political reality capable of generating genuine change in their lives?

The situation allowed no sitting back, not a minute could be lost: political timing is one of the most important variables at any historical juncture. And that is what it was, a crucial point at which the existence of the revolutionary project was at stake.

The government had to make advances, starting from an unavoidable premise: as a consequence of opposition actions, Venezuela's GDP had dropped by more than 20 percent during 2002, unemployment had increased by almost 25 percent, real wages significantly diminished, only a few thousand homes were built, and basic goods were beyond the reach of millions of people. Hunger, begging, and violence were all on the increase. Despite the fact that resources assigned to education and health had doubled since 1999, setbacks or stagnation had settled in both sectors, after certain successes. Successes included the creation of 2,000 new-style Bolivarian schools, with full-day sessions and three meals a day for students; and the reduction in the infant mortality rate by nearly four points (from 22 to 18 per thousand live births). Nevertheless, illiteracy remained at the same level, the revolution was barely making itself felt in the rest of the education sector, and public health services could not be sustained.

It was essential to act quickly and create benefits within the reach of the largest possible number of poor people, to show them with concrete examples that the revolution they had mobilized and fought for in April, and ardently backed in December, had social and economic content in addition to political and moral strength. But, speaking honestly, an immediate economic leap was not possible, first because structural burdens required slower policies and strategic planning, and second, because events between the end of 2001 and January 2003 had caused a significant recession. The only possible immediate action—which was taken—was to restore oil production and thus reestablish the flow of financial resources indispensable for taking the social and economic offensive.

Furthermore, the revolution could not fail to take the offensive in the political field. In spite of the two major setbacks it suffered in April and in December, the opposition's financial resources were virtually intact, and it had the support of the private media and encouragement and backing from President Bush. It was planning a new stage: getting rid of Chávez by means of a recall referendum, which could feasibly be set in motion at the end of 2003 or in early 2004. Their calculations could not have been more cynical: to utilize the widespread discontent in broad sectors of the population—dissatisfaction caused by the crisis generated by that very opposition. Failing to get rid of Chávez by unconstitutional means, the counterrevolution decided to achieve that end within the framework of the constitution. This scenario was highly risky for Chávez, as a reasonable number of his less-aware followers were susceptible to manipulation, a fact confirmed by reliable opinion polls.

ORIGINS

At that crossroads of tension and hope, doubt and affirmation, Barrio Adentro (Inside the Barrio, or Inside Marginal Neighborhoods) and the other social missions leapt into existence in the course of 2003—and since then. They have become the most significant, fundamental events of the Bolivarian revolution after the political gains in 1999 (the new constitution), 2000 (Chávez's reelection), and 2001 (the passing of basic laws, like the land reform and hydrocarbon laws). These social programs are authentic Venezuelan initiatives, and are unprecedented in any other Latin American country—including Cuba, where exceptional advances in health and education took more time to organize—in terms of their reach, originality, daring, speed, and popular and military participation.

From March 2003 the social missions began to flow like fresh spring water and between July 1 and November of that year almost all of them were well established and underway. President Chávez formulated the broader concept of the social missions while organizing the battle against illiteracy in May 2003. That battle was the most appropriate response to a decisive question: how to bring together and direct all the actors who could make the eradication of illiteracy in Venezuela a possibility in less than 18 months? The president identified two principal support bases: the forces of civil society most committed to the Bolivarian process, and the military, which could provide significant logistical backing. He also decided not to hand over direction of the task to the traditional state bureaucracy, but incorporated from it what was available and most needed—for example, material resources and cadres. The task was then given to the direction of the new being itself: the social missions. These began to operate without formalistic schemes or compromises and with a unified, and dynamic pressure—a result of the desire to achieve effective, rapid results. They unleashed broad participation within a large part of the population, who on noting and trusting the visible advances developed greater and greater enthusiasm.

Mission Robinson (the literacy campaign) was the pioneer of the social missions—its formal and active launch took place on July 1, 2003, prior to its conception and initial organization in May. There were two precedents to the missions in March and April, linked to what would later be christened Mission MERCAL (nutrition) and Barrio Adentro (health), the latter being the most famous and popular of all the missions.

As an antidote to the shortage of foodstuffs caused by the December 2002 oil strike, President Hugo Chávez realized that the government needed to create a powerful system for the wholesale purchase of foodstuffs and their retail distribution at prices accessible to the low-income population. In March, a commercial network was established that, via thousands of retailers—of different sizes—could sell essential products to people at lower prices than on the private market. So, within a short space of time, Mission MERCAL came into existence.

On April 16, 2003, the first 58 Cuban doctors who were to launch Barrio Adentro arrived in Caracas. At that point, the mission was in its embryonic, experimental form. Those people who initially drew up the program could never have imagined what would happen subsequently. President Chávez, however, was planning a similar program but on a national scale. So in May he met with those 58 Cuban doctors and the mayor of Caracas, Freddy Bernal, to redesign the project and transform it into practical action.

And, in May 2003, President Chávez also decided to ask Fidel Castro for support in utilizing the Cuban "Yes, I Can" teaching method in order to eradicate illiteracy in 12 months [which developed into Mission Robinson]. A pilot project was immediately organized and coordinated by the armed forces in Caracas, Aragua, and Vargas, and was highly successful. On the same organizational basis, the Venezuelan president set up three new educational missions in the second half of the year: education up to sixth grade, secondary education, and university education.

An interesting aspect of the social missions is their identity. Chávez has not only been their principal architect, he has also assigned them their names, associating each mission with a famous Venezuelan patriot. Missions Robinson I (the literacy campaign) and II (sixth grade) became rapidly known by their name—the pseudonym used by Simón Bolívar's teacher, Simón Rodríguez. The name Barrio Adentro immediately caught on within the country and internationally, especially after the impact of the program in the hills of Caracas where the country's most recognizably poor live. The names of other missions were similarly popular: Mission Ribas (secondary school education), named in honor of the youthful independence martyr José Félix Ribas; Mission Sucre, invoking Antonio José de Sucre, the grand marshal of Ayacucho; Mission MERCAL, the initials of the food markets; and Mission Vuelvan Caras, named after the historic victory of General Páez and his troops over the Spanish royalists.

The social missions were formally launched at public events presided over by President Chávez, on the following days:

- Mission Robinson I: July 1, 2003
- Mission Robinson II: October 28, 2003
- Mission Sucre: November 3, 2003
- Mission Ribas: November 17, 2003
- Mission Barrio Adentro: December 14, 2003
- Mission MERCAL: January 2004

Mission Vuelvan Caras (to generate employment and stimulate autonomous economic development via cooperatives), Mission Identidad (giving of identity cards to 5,076,660 Venezuelans and registering 1,232,000 on the voter lists), and Mission Hábitat (designed to resolve the housing deficit in 10 years), likewise emerged in 2004.

In this introduction, I refer to the missions that came into existence in 2003 and 2004, which became the engine of the new stage of the Bolivarian revolution. They represent the principal dynamic factors that made recent great Bolivarian victories possible: the recall referendum of August 15, 2004, and the regional elections of October 30, 2004, in which the revolution won 20 of the 22 states in dispute and more than 75 percent of the mayoralties.

WHAT ARE THE SOCIAL MISSIONS?

The social missions emerged at a historic crossroads in the Bolivarian process, out of the search for genuine solutions to the grave social and economic problems of Venezuela's poor, who total more than 17 million of the country's 25 million inhabitants.

They are based on a new relationship between the state and civil society and can claim the broadest and most effective participation of the people in solving their own difficulties. The missions are at the center of the Bolivarian government's policy to combat poverty without respite, in a fundamental and decisive way. They are formed around President Chávez's concept of granting power to the poor so they become protagonists in their own emancipation and can gain more power and fortify their principal role in the defense, support, and development of the Bolivarian revolution. In that sense, the social missions represent a decisive historical stage in the advance and consolidation of the Bolivarian process. The Bolivarian revolution has been able to crystallize its democratic and popular nature thanks to the social missions and, to a significant degree, its future development depends on their effectiveness.

The social missions are the direct beneficiaries of the new blueprint for distributing oil profits in a just way. They are not programs simply seeking short-term palliative solutions, and while they might continue to develop partially or totally in the future, they are already achieving definitive solutions for the poor.

State institutions are participating in their organization and leadership but the missions are not subordinated to traditional bureaucratic structures. Each mission has its own profile and a notable degree of creativity, its ultimate aim being to meet the human rights enshrined in the Bolivarian constitution without formalism or excuses. In the fields of health, education, housing, employment, nutrition, sports, and culture, among others, the missions are run in such a way that they embody a primordial force for fulfilling the 1999 constitution; they represent its raison d'être. They are aimed at transforming an inherited legacy and, at the same time, establishing new legal standards in tune with the imperatives of revolutionary change.

For President Chávez, "these social missions are the nucleus of the strategic offensive to progressively reduce poverty, to give power to the poor. That is their challenge, to solve old ills and simultaneously create the structural conditions to facilitate

the construction of a new society, in which everyone will be members with equal rights and duties."
How will the social missions allow the poor to gain power? Let us examine Barrio Adentro, Robinson I and II, Ribas, Sucre, and MERCAL, to evaluate their strategic advances within the Bolivarian revolution.

BARRIO ADENTRO:
A GENERAL HEALTH MISSION

Prior to Barrio Adentro, the health panorama in Venezuela was similar to that of other Latin American nations, with the exception of Cuba. More than 17 million Venezuelan people were excluded from general medical attention and wide sectors of the middle class were suffering—and still are—from the onslaught of the privatization and commercialization of health services.

The figure of 58 Cuban doctors who arrived in the poor barrios of Caracas in April 2003 quickly swelled in the following months, to the point where they were providing health care for all the poor citizens of Caracas. From July, the program was extended to the rest of Venezuela and between October and November alone more than 4,000 Cuban health professionals arrived. On December 14, 2003, when President Chávez formally announced the launch of Barrio Adentro, it had already expanded to almost all corners of the country, and was being operated by 10,179 Cuban doctors, hundreds of nurses, and some Venezuelan physicians.

The Venezuelan Medical Federation—a fanatical defender of the commercialization of health care—opposed from the outset this new, revolutionary, and humanist mode of caring for the health of the poor, and with the private media's grotesque support unleashed a furious campaign against the Cuban doctors.

The results of the doctors' work, however, and their willingness to live among the poor and attend people on a 24-hour basis, in their homes, ensured the resounding failure of the campaign: it was rejected by the overwhelming majority of the population. Even political opposition leaders were deciding to seek medical treatment from the Cuban doctors and were refraining from criticizing such an altruistic mission and its popularity.

Barrio Adentro is based on a concept of general health, combining both primary and preventive care, placing emphasis on educating people and gaining their support in averting the causes of illnesses. This is made possible by doctors actually living in communities and is supported by the work of local health committees, which have rapidly proliferated throughout the country. Barrio Adentro is linked with work around sports, nutrition, the environment, social economy, culture, and education. It is important to note that the vast majority of the doctors began their work in improvised consulting rooms, either in the houses where they were living or nearby, and almost always in cramped and difficult conditions. In spite of the fact that the president assigned resources to build consulting rooms and fit them with the necessary furniture and equipment, this has not occurred quickly due to serious bureaucratic shortcomings (that are being addressed in 2005). However, thanks to the generous and creative support of the population, practical solutions were found that have guaranteed the doctors' daily labor.

One innovative aspect of this mission is the free dispensing of medicine to every patient attended by a doctor. The doctors have access to about 100 medicines with which they can treat about 95 percent of common ailments.

In this way, Barrio Adentro was meeting the preventive and primary care needs of 17 million people, with a total of approximately 14,000 doctors (one to every 250 families). Once this was accomplished, two new services were initiated. From late 2003 into mid-2004, free dental and eye care was established throughout the country, which includes ophthalmology services and the provision of free glasses, and 3,019 dental and 459 optical chairs. The services similarly covered 17 million poor people. One outstanding aspect of the dental service is the incorporation of some 1,200 young Venezuelan professionals, who work in an integrated, fraternal way with 3,000 Cuban colleagues and, at the same time, study with those Cubans to reach specialist level.

Barrio Adentro's next step was the experimental installation of 84 diagnostic centers in the states of Miranda, Zulia, Carabobo, Táchira, and Caracas. In September–October 2004, these centers began to offer free electrocardiographic, endoscopic, ultrasound, X-ray, and laboratory services. In 2005 there are plans to extend these diagnostic services to all poor people throughout the country, likewise free of charge. Their results have been so successful that President Chávez has asked Cuba to provide these services to the middle class.

Not stopping there, in July 2004, in coordination with the Barrio Adentro doctors, one of the most noble, generous social programs ever conceived emerged: Mission Milagro (Miracle). Milagro guarantees free surgery in Cuba for all Venezuelans suffering from cataract and other eye disorders. The service includes transportation, board, and lodging for the patients and covers the same costs for a companion, if needed. In less than six months, more than 20,000 people have had their sight restored. In 2005, another 100,000 patients with visual difficulties are to be treated. Describing it as a "miracle" has been no exaggeration.

Other interesting statistics confirm the efficiency and success of Barrio Adentro: on average, the Cuban doctors give 6.4 million consultations every month. They visit 1.22 million families, direct 3.9 million education activities, and save close to 1,000 lives. In a similar month, Cuban and Venezuelan dental surgeons offer 720,000 consultations, do 680,000 fillings and 160,000 extractions, carry out 710,000 education activities, and conduct 210,000 checks for mouth cancer. For their part, opticians examine an average of 188,000 people per month, also supplying the required glasses.

One final, significant figure: within the Barrio Adentro program there were 76 million consultations in the year 2004 alone, while in the five-year period 1994–98 there were barely 70 million consultations within the entire Venezuelan public health system. Of course, and well and truly beyond statistics, the fundamental aspect of Barrio Adentro is the quality of the medical care, the fact that it is free, its preventive focus, and the tremendous psychological security felt by people previously excluded who now have the guarantee of a family doctor within their immediate reach.

BARRIO ADENTRO II: ANOTHER EXCEPTIONAL HEALTH PROGRAM

One valuable experience for the Barrio Adentro doctors concerned patients for whom further diagnosis was necessary. On many occasions patients could not afford this and never received further tests, as diagnostic services in the public sector are insufficient, or nonexistent.

Positive trials in the 84 initial diagnostic centers confirmed the need to offer these services to everyone within the Barrio Adentro program. Furthermore, President Chávez decided to extend these services to the country as a whole, offering them to everyone. That concept of universal access gave rise to another daring, exceptional idea: the creation of a secondary health system not just in diagnostics but in intensive care and emergency services, capable of saving the lives of 100,000 people every year; and the establishment of another secondary health system for rehabilitation and physiotherapy. Both would have nationwide coverage.

President Chávez christened the new combination of services Barrio Adentro II and took advantage of his annual speech to the National Assembly to announce it, indicating it would be fully in place by March 2005.

When I heard the details of this huge leap into the future, I couldn't help but exclaim: "It sounds like science fiction!" Yet, under the personal direction of the president, intensive work is already underway on the project, with close coordination between Cuban doctors and other specialists and diverse Venezuelan institutions.

Barrio Adentro II will very soon become reality, transcending Venezuela's borders to become an example of what an excellent health system—free to all people—could and should be.

Barrio Adentro II includes:

- 600 general diagnostic centers (CDI) with 24-hour emergency and intensive care services, 150 of them with emergency operating theaters. They are able to provide X-ray, laboratory, and ultrasound services; microanalytic systems to detect viral and congenital diseases; and endoscopic, electrocardiographic, and ophthalmology facilities.
- 35 hi-tech diagnostic centers (one in each of the country's states and two or three in larger states), with cutting-edge diagnostic equipment that, in conjunction with the CDIs, facilitates the accurate detection or diagnosis of most illnesses. Each center will have facilities for CAT scans, MRI scans, non-invasive ultrasound, videoendoscopy, and mammography and floating X-ray units, among other services.
- 600 rehabilitation and physiotherapy rooms, with electrotherapy, thermotherapy, hydrotherapy, occupational therapy, natural and traditional medicine, podiatry, gymnasium facilities, and services for speech and hearing disorders.

The impact of Barrio Adentro II on the Venezuelan public and private health systems remains to be seen. It is expected to have a positive influence within the public sector, prompting essential changes, and allowing hospitals to fulfill their important role, and to complete an excellent combination of health services based on general primary care.

BARRIO ADENTRO AND TRAINING NEW HEALTH PROFESSIONALS

One innovative and significant contribution of Barrio Adentro is the training of 40,000 Venezuelan doctors over the next 10 years. There will be direct links between students and doctors involved in the missions, both I and II.

It is an iconoclastic concept of education, and is a new way of training general community doctors with reliable professional and practical experience and in the essential ethics of serving people rather than using patients for personal gain.

Within this scheme, every Cuban doctor works with a small group of students. The students learn with audiovisual materials and in computer classes, and the Cuban physicians act as guides, facilitators, and trainers in the consulting rooms, the Barrio Adentro II facilities, and in daily contact with the population. At the same time, 5,000 students will be trained to university level as technicians, to handle the equipment in the diagnostic and rehabilitation centers.

In a few years, Venezuela will have enough doctors to replace their Cuban counterparts and will even be able to accompany the latter on other Barrio Adentro missions elsewhere in the Americas.

SPORTS IN BARRIO ADENTRO

In an important component of Barrio Adentro, in April 2003 a group of Cuban professionals in sports and physical recreation began to work in the Libertador municipality of Caracas. For the first time in those barrios many children, adults, and senior citizens had the possibility of participating in sports, undertaking physical education, or organizing themselves to practice basic gymnastics, dance therapy, or other activities. The success of the program was so resounding that it was soon extended to the whole country and today these coaches are offering their services to anyone living in poor areas who is interested. There are currently 8,250 sports teachers in the mission, at a ratio of one to approximately 2,200 people. Like the doctors, these professionals live with people in the barrios and, with the support of the population, are making it possible for people to practice sports in open or covered areas. Each teacher works with one or two young Venezuelan sports workers and has close links with the Barrio Adentro doctors, who support them in rehabilitation treatment, developing exercise programs for pregnant women, etc.

In summary, the program of sports, and a culture of physical recreation in the context of Barrio Adentro, has become an innovative way to improve the quality of life of millions of people.

THE EDUCATIONAL MISSIONS

When Hugo Chávez assumed the presidency in February 1999, the state of public education in Venezuela was horrific. The school attendance rate stood at just 59 percent, there were 1.5 million illiterates, more than two million adults who had only reached sixth grade, and close to a further two million who had been unable to complete their secondary education. The situation was compounded by the more than 500,000 secondary school graduates who could not find a place at university, which had virtually become the preserve of students from private schools. The quality of teaching was steadily deteriorating, and the education budget was at barely 2.8 percent of GDP.

The revolutionary government adopted very important measures during 1999–2001: it created 2,000 Bolivarian schools with full-day sessions, increased the education budget to more than 5 percent of GDP, and prohibited enrollment charges in public schools. Excluded children began to be incorporated into the education system. Teachers' salaries were raised and their work recognized as truly important.

The major transformation of the education system, however, occurred in 2003 with Missions Robinson I and II, Mission Ribas, and Mission Sucre.

These Venezuelan educational missions represent a landmark in Latin American and Caribbean educational policies. Each mission has in common the use of audiovisual teaching aids and the central role of facilitators. Facilitators serve as mediators between video classes that are prerecorded by excellent teachers, and the students, who watch and participate in those lessons together. This method has worked successfully in all the educational missions; it guarantees the homogeneity of each course as well as high-quality educational content that is both attractive and accessible to the average student. It has been demonstrated at all levels of education that the critical mass of knowledge acquired by the students is very high, due in large part to the video classes that illustrate explanations and information.

MISSION ROBINSON

Mission Robinson was the pioneer in this new educational concept.

A pilot project was run in May–June 2003, which demonstrated the effectiveness of the Cuban literacy method "Yes,

I Can." Based on 65 audiovisual classes, the course makes it possible for illiterate students to learn to read and write in seven weeks. In May, President Chávez formed the national Presidential Literacy Commission, and others at the state and municipal levels, composed of officials from the ministries of Education, Culture, and Energy and Mines; officers from the armed forces; managers of PDVSA (the national oil company); and governors and mayors. The commissions were bound to act with the backing of grassroots popular organizations. On July 1 Mission Robinson was launched, which covered urban barrios, and the plains, jungle, and mountains. Hundreds of thousands of patriots (as the students were called) joined the project and in December of that year it was announced one million Venezuelans had attained literacy. The mission was virtually fulfilled by the end of 2004. The mission's success entailed organizing 78,957 study areas nationally, with 80,000 televisions and video players, plus more than 100,000 facilitators and supervisors—civilian and military—who received a monthly wage equivalent to $100 for transportation and food costs.

This noble labor of love and culture was carried out with great joy and popular participation. Chávez's aim to give power to the poor through knowledge was put into practice. Poor people, even those with least access to education traditionally, immediately joined up and proved the idea was valid. The literacy teachers, many of them young people or housewives, benefited from their diverse experiences and the moral and spiritual gains, as well as acquiring a fuller comprehension of the revolutionary process.

Various obstacles presented themselves. The televisions, videos, cassettes, readers, notebooks, and pencils had to be distributed over almost one million square kilometers. The armed forces guaranteed the success of this extraordinary logistical task, providing land, air, and river transportation and access to barracks storerooms. Without that coverage, it would have been impossible to create the mission's material base. During the pilot study in May, it became clear that many pupils could not see the texts, and a program for eye tests for all those with problems was quickly instigated, which resulted in giving glasses to 300,000 people. When students abandoned the classes for various reasons, they were visited at home and persuaded to rejoin. All those who graduated were given a family library of 25 books. The most outstanding students received encouragement in the form of credits, housing, and jobs.

Mission Robinson signified the unleashing of hope and potential. A 68-year-old woman affirmed emotionally to President Chávez during the graduation ceremony: "I thought of that saying 'an old parrot can't learn to talk,' but these classes are a miracle!" She was referring to the Cuban "Yes, I Can!" teaching method, which was made significantly Venezuelan. Through Mission Robinson, the method demonstrated that it is indeed possible to incorporate poor people into the educational revolution and represented an unprecedented explosion of motivation and participation, which would continue building with the other educational missions, through which the most excluded could reaffirm that, in fact, they could advance toward the light of knowledge.

MISSION ROBINSON II

Even before Mission Robinson started, an education program had been conceived to ensure that those who had learned to read and write, and other adults whose education was terminated before sixth grade, could reach that level. It also used audiovisual materials and relied on the guidance of facilitators. The "Yes, I Can Go On" teaching method emerged from the experiences of the application in Venezuela of the "Yes, I Can" method, and guarantees sixth-grade education in two consecutive years of study, including English and computer studies.

Mission Robinson II was formally launched on October 28, 2003, and within a few months had an intake of 1.2 million pupils, more than 60 percent of them recently literate.

MISSION RIBAS

This new mission, aimed at making it possible for more than one million adults to complete secondary school education, was similarly a great success. Within a few weeks of its inauguration on November 17, 2003, more than 800,000 people had joined the project. This time the logistical support, organization, and direction of the mission was assigned to the Ministry of Energy and Mines and the state oil company PDVSA, as confirmation of their new role in serving the interests of the people. That decision also encouraged a greater ethical and political commitment to the Bolivarian process on the part of officials and workers at PDVSA.

The new mission adopted audiovisual teaching methods, and was similarly based on a close and fruitful cooperation between Venezuelan and Cuban specialists. They organized a system of education in the areas of science, humanities, and technology, to guarantee school-leaving certificates in just two years.

MISSION SUCRE

One Sunday a survey was organized to take place in all the country's public plazas—which filled to overflowing—to discover the approximate number of school leavers without university places. The result: more than half a million. In order to incorporate such a large number of school leavers into higher studies, the decision was made to move forward in stages and in groups. Prior to entering university, each group would undertake a preparatory course aimed at refreshing and consolidating students' knowledge.

One fundamental aspect of Mission Sucre is the concept of the municipalization of higher education: in other words, to create university courses where students are living, and to create courses in line with the needs of each region and the country. It presupposes a departure from the narrow confines of university education—where classes are given in historic buildings and led by professors. That set-up is replaced with more modest premises, video classes, and professional facilitators who are trained in this context.

A few months before that Sunday, on July 30, President Chávez announced plans for Mission Sucre and the municipalization of universities. On the same day, he inaugurated the first headquarters of the Bolivarian University—the former, luxurious offices of the oil technocrats and servants of the oligarchy and foreign capital—where studies in legal science, history, and communications are now taking place.

400,000 SCHOLARSHIPS FOR THE POOR

One of the most innovative and striking attributes of the educational missions is the creation of 400,000 scholarships for the poorest students: 200,000 within Robinson II and 100,000 within Ribas and Sucre respectively. These scholarships consist of grants equivalent to $100 per month (70 percent of the minimum wage) and represent encouragement and real support, providing basic conditions so that recipients can undertake their studies. They also represent a genuine reduction in unemployment.

MISSION MERCAL: GUARANTEED NUTRITION FOR THE POOR

The embryo of this great program dates back to the mass distress at the shortages caused by the oil strike of December 2002 and January 2003. Then, President Chávez decided to instigate a vast, state-run entrepreneurial system to guarantee the people's food sovereignty by eliminating hunger and contributing to the improved nutrition of Venezuela's poor.

Today, Mission MERCAL—finally launched in January 2004—is a palpable reality. It benefits more than 10 million people with subsidized foodstuffs (at an average of 25 percent below market prices), or free to those with no resources. The commercial establishments of the MERCAL network are everywhere. Food kitchens have been organized in the poor barrios—each offering free lunches and afternoon snacks to about 150 people—and benefiting more than 900,000 people across the country, increasing this year to cover more than one million.

There is the extraordinary idea of converting these food kitchens into places where, in addition to food, people can receive health and educational attention and join in recreational, cultural, and sporting activities. That work is being undertaken with the support of the young members of the Francisco de Miranda Social Workers Front, who under the guidance of President Chávez are working cooperatively and methodically within all the country's poor barrios.

There is also the maximum security program that grants a 50 percent subsidy on the price of seven essential items, currently benefiting two million people.

It is a fact that a food program of such reach and characteristics has never been previously organized in any Latin American country. Mission MERCAL is a reference point of much interest to other countries, because it demonstrates the feasibility of counteracting the disastrous effects of neoliberalism and, instead, demonstrates the correct role of governments in the social distribution of wealth, if those governments really are committed to being democratic and sovereign nations.

In summary, MERCAL is making a tremendous contribution to the immediate problem of hunger and malnutrition. Moreover, thanks to the existence of the other social and economic programs with which it interacts, it is developing with a broad perspective.

CUBAN PARTICIPATION IN BARRIO ADENTRO AND THE EDUCATIONAL MISSIONS

The following questions and responses have been drawn from several interviews conducted with Germán Sánchez between June 2003 and April 2005.

CUBA IN BARRIO ADENTRO

Are the Cuban doctors participating in Barrio Adentro really physicians, or have they just come here to indoctrinate our people?

Your question is opportune, because it allows me to refer to one of the most widespread lies in relation to the Cuban doctors who are offering their services in the poor barrios of Caracas. Ever since the arrival in 1999 of the first Cuban health contingent, to help people affected by the landslide in Vargas, members of the Venezuelan Medical Federation and other spokespeople for similarly questionable causes have charged our doctors at best with being untrained professionals come to take jobs away from Venezuelan doctors or, at worst, with being undercover agents. They said then—and are reiterating this now—that the real role of the Cuban doctors was to politicize people in favor of President Chávez. It was slanderous then—in the face of a natural disaster—and is now, in the face of the social disaster the Cuban doctors have come to confront.

With respect, I would suggest that your question can be answered by the 17 million citizens who have benefited from the thorough, daily work—at any hour—of our doctors, all of whom are highly qualified, and educated with the philosophy to serve human beings rather than profit from them. The first thing those humble Venezuelans say is that nobody can ever take that medical attention away from them. Our doctors are contributing to combating the horrendous image that existed of those communities, which are doubtless weighed down with problems and inequalities, but at the same time are rich with humanism and the capacity to welcome anyone who has decided to offer them solidarity, and aid, without deception.

No Cuban doctor will ever become involved in Venezuelan politics. Their work is strictly professional. Naturally, they are the bearers of the values and ideas of our people. I ask myself: Are the schemers afraid of the Venezuelan people's access to these opinions? As Cubans, we are certain of our historical direction and whether in Cuba or in any corner of the planet we are disposed to talk about our social realities.

Why is Cuba sending so many doctors to Venezuela? Wouldn't it be better if they remain on the island, where there are huge health problems?

The presence of Cuban doctors in Bolívar's homeland is nothing out of the ordinary. Firstly, we are paying a historic debt of gratitude to the first nation that taught us the course of freedom and independence and always acted in solidarity with us. Cuba has close to 70,000 doctors, one for every 160 people, the highest ratio in the world. For years now, our physicians have been lending their services in many countries, in places where medical attention is not available and where governments have requested it. Prior to the Barrio Adentro experience more than

53,000 health professionals and technicians have worked in 93 countries. At present, not counting Venezuela, approximately 4,000 doctors are working in 22 countries, and have saved the lives of more than 461,000 people. More than 500 health workers are offering their services in countries such as Guatemala and Haiti. In all those places, they work voluntarily and with altruism, without receiving a salary from their host nation, and neither do those governments pay Cuba any fees. Our country guarantees their salaries and takes responsibility for the quality and ethics of their work. They respect the customs and laws of those nations. No other country in the world trains doctors in the vocation of solidarity and it is a matter of pride and satisfaction for our health professionals to help other peoples who are suffering great hardship.

In relation to the Cuban health service, it makes more sense to talk figures: average life expectancy is 77 years, the infant mortality rate is 5.8 per 1,000 live births. The entire population has access to free preventive attention and high-quality care. No one in Cuba is suffering or dying from lack of medical attention. All citizens are given several vaccinations; our country manufactures 70 percent of the medicines it consumes and some of its hi-tech equipment; thousands of scientists are researching cancer, HIV/AIDS, and developing new vaccines and cutting-edge medicines; illnesses such as polio, diphtheria, tetanus, measles, German measles, meningitis, mumps, hemophilia, and hepatitis have been eradicated or controlled. We are producing vaccines against meningitis, hepatitis B, leprosy, tetanus, and diphtheria, among others. Currently, research trials of vaccines against cholera (which does not exist on the island), tuberculosis, and other strains of hepatitis and meningitis are underway, as well as pneumonia and Alzheimer's disease. We have more than 2,500 scientists working in human health research, and they are supported by advanced scientific and technological resources.

Suffice to say, for example, that European and US companies

have 52 projects for developing anti-cancer vaccines and Cuba—alone—has nine, four of them at the stage of clinical trials. Moreover, we are advancing on various congenital disease programs: in 1982 we were the second country in the world to have a diagnostic and prenatal prevention plan for congenital malformations, and cretinism was eliminated in 1986, thanks to the congenital hypothyroid program. Our scientists have invented technology that can detect and measure auditory problems before children are born.

In summary, the Cuban health strategy combines both an efficient system of primary care centered around family doctors, with the use of the latest technologies, medicines, and vaccines. It is sustained by excellent scientific research and a developed pharmaceutical industry.

Between these two extremes, we have 267 hospitals and 444 polyclinics, which are currently being renovated and improved. Cuba will soon be the country with the finest and most modern health system for all people at an international level. This advance in our health services means we expect to attain an average life expectancy of 80 within five years.

How many doctors is Cuba thinking of sending to Venezuela?

Our commitment is to cover the primary care needs of all poor families at the rate of one doctor to 1,200 citizens. There are currently some 14,000 general physicians and just over 3,000 dentists.

Cuba has many more doctors ready to fulfill this noble and historic mission in any part of Venezuela. All of them are specialists in general medicine and have an average experience of more than 10 years. This semester [2005] a further 6,000 new doctors, technical personnel, and other professionals are to begin work in the 600 diagnostic centers and rehabilitation rooms and the 35 hi-tech diagnostic centers.

High-level training and professional experience complement

the ethics and humanism of our doctors. No country in the world trains doctors with a double education in ethics and professionalism, doctors who are then capable of fulfilling their duty in any circumstances or location on the planet. That is what prompts amazement and admiration for our doctors. They are outstanding in their humility, dedication, and satisfaction at having achieved their work. This is even more so the case in Venezuela, because all the doctors know they are part of a unique experience in Latin America: for the first time, the poorest sectors of a country are receiving high-quality, comprehensive health care, and this will soon be the case for the rest of the population.

Our intention is not to replace Venezuelan doctors, but the reverse; it is about collaborating to obtain accelerated results for the entire population; to drastically reduce its morbidity and mortality rates. We are sure this experience will become a paradigm of worldwide interest and impact. Hopefully our doctors will soon begin to be replaced by their Venezuelan colleagues and, in the not too distant future, unite efforts to help our sisters and brothers in Brazil, Ecuador, Colombia, and other nations of Latin America. Cuba's commitment is to help train 40,000 Venezuela doctors within 10 years. The first 20,000 young students are about to start their community medical courses. A further 20,000 young Venezuelans are to study medicine in Cuba, living throughout the country in the homes of Cuban families.

Why have there been such bad practices on the part of Cuban doctors?

In fact, the bad practice has been committed on the part of certain media and officials in health trade unions and institutions—it is they who have displayed a lack of ethics.

In all the cases of so-called bad practice that have been investigated and exposed, it has been irrefutably demonstrated that these were publicity stunts to discredit our doctors, promote fear among the population, generate a public rejection of Barrio Adentro, and cause the failure of the health program. These macabre stunts were lead by directors of professional institutions—like the Venezuelan Medical Federation—and [private] hospitals, which have lied to the Venezuelan people and displayed a total absence of professionalism toward their Cuban colleagues. It is remarkable that almost all the leaders of the political opposition parties have said very little and have not really joined in these campaigns. Is that possibly because they are aware of the real impact of the labor of our doctors on millions of people? We have remained calm in the face of such insults, because the people have not let themselves be confused.

CUBA IN THE EDUCATIONAL MISSIONS

Let's change the subject. I would like to know why Cuba selected Venezuela for the "Yes, I Can" literacy teaching method.

It was the other way around. President Chávez was aware of the existence of this highly innovative method and talked with Fidel to implement it in Venezuela. It all happened very quickly. Fidel first publicly described the method in his 2003 May Day speech. Then, in the first week of May, he personally presented Chávez with the course videos. Within 24 hours, Chávez had viewed the tapes and made the decision to organize a giant literacy campaign. He recognized the educational quality of the course and correctly perceived that it could be successfully adapted to Venezuelan realities. He quickly came up with the name Mission Robinson—very Venezuelan—created the Presidential Literacy Commission and other leadership structures and gave instructions to the armed forces to undertake a pilot scheme with 400 illiterate people. He also proposed the goal: to teach one million people to read and write by the end of the year and to eliminate illiteracy during 2004.

Of course, Fidel, the Cubans working on developing the new method, and all of us—the Cuban people—accepted President Chávez's appeal with great enthusiasm and honor.

Venezuela has exceptional conditions for the development of a literacy program of such magnitude. As far as I know, at the present time it could not be achieved in any other Latin American country, even one with similar geography and numbers of illiterates (1.5 million). Why can it be achieved in Venezuela? First, because a process of profound social work and high degree of popular participation is evolving here; second, because of the doctrine of the armed forces—the defense of sovereignty based on equity and social justice—and its experience of direct action to the benefit of communities, which dates back to 1999 [the Vargas landslide]; and third, the fact that the nation's president has the humanism and leadership to direct a civil-military mission of great magnitude and complexity. There are two further reasons: the years of intense struggles have produced social leaders and thousands of people prepared to take on responsibilities of that magnitude without any desire for personal gain; and due to various factors, the government's social agenda had fallen behind and so since 2003 President Chávez has been pushing it forward with great speed. We have no doubts: Venezuela is already the first country in the South to have succeeded in eradicating illiteracy in the early years of the 21st century. Moreover, it has done so in a very short period of time, converting Mission Robinson into a global reference point and Venezuela into the second Latin American country free of illiteracy.

Who guarantees the method's effectiveness?

Mission Robinson has not only been successful in terms of the

Cuban "Yes, I Can" method. Its educational quality is unquestionable. Its methodology is based on the relationship between numbers and letters; in other words, it is based on illiterate people's knowledge of numbers, and then advances toward learning letters, syllables, and words. It is simple and rapid. Audiovisual material is made comprehensible and attractive. The video classes demonstrate a teacher working with a group of students—in reality, Cuban actors—who, in 65 half-hour classes, also using the primer, learn to write and write. The classes are animated and reinforced with images, attractive texts, and commentaries on diverse themes. The real students, in groups of up to 10, observe each class, and are guided by a facilitator. With two classes every day, students learn to read and write in seven weeks.

Cuba's authority in literacy work is nothing new. In 1961 our people eliminated illiteracy in eight months, using a traditional literacy manual and primer, utilizing the mass participation of young people who lived with those they were teaching. That experience was unprecedented and was never repeated in other countries. Cuba became a paradigm for specialized literacy institutions and a source of inspiration and experience for other countries.

Out of a desire to help other peoples, our country recently developed a radio literacy teaching method, successful in some of the countries where it has been applied; more than 300,000 people have learned to read and write in that way. The "Yes, I Can" method is the result of a secular experience and the sound foundation of our pedagogy, which has received five UNESCO prizes for its contribution to literacy.

It is very important to highlight the adaptation of that method which has taken place in Venezuela. Various contributions and changes have already been made, such as the percentage of pupils to facilitators, and in the guiding and complementary role of the latter. One tremendous example of the creativity of the Venezuelan teachers is the application of the Cuban method to Braille language for the blind.

"Yes, I Can" possesses undoubted merits, but we should recognize that its success in Venezuela is a consequence of the responsible, enthusiastic, and widely participative manner in which it has been implemented and adapted, without recourse to nationalist concepts and at the same time with a restrained and balanced Venezuelan imprint.

In real terms, how many literacy teachers did Cuba send?

When President Chávez mentioned that Mission Robinson was to use a Cuban teaching method, it was as if he stepped on a nest of snakes. I heard on radio, saw on television, and read in newspapers so many ill-intentioned comments and twisted speculations that I felt it would be wise not to make any statement and wait until the facts could speak for themselves. And that's how it was. Those who argued about the presence of thousands of Cuban literacy teachers, about indoctrination methods, who said that Cuba had no contribution to make in the field of literacy, and other nonsense, were soon silenced. The results are irrefutable. Will they learn their lesson? Will they finally realize that Cuba is not the hell they paint it to be, or the backwater they attempt to make it seem in order to frighten and confuse the naïve? Will they need a special Mission Robinson to teach them literacy in ethics and professionalism?

Our human contribution to Mission Robinson has been what Venezuela requested: three advisors for each state and 11 at national level, all highly qualified individuals who feel a strong spirit of cooperation.

Other aid, on Fidel's initiative, has been to provide a significant proportion of the mission's technical base: televisions, video recorders, readers, facilitator manuals, cassettes of recorded classes, prescription glasses, and ophthalmic equipment with the relevant technical personnel. As Cubans we feel proud, because we know that our contribution will result in one of the most significant events in the history of education in Venezuela and the world.

Is Cuba to continue supporting Venezuela in Mission Robinson II (sixth grade) and in other education programs like Missions Sucre and Ribas?

Yes, we are prepared to do that. Venezuelan–Cuban coordination in Mission Robinson has been a complete success and that gives us an even greater commitment to the Venezuelan people to work on other educational projects of similar reach with the country's educationalists. Moreover, we feel that this Venezuelan-Cuban educational alliance, with mutual respect for the identity and decisions of both nations, will have repercussions in other places and, in passing, our specialists are also learning a tremendous amount here. Together we can extend our bilateral experiences to help other Latin American and Caribbean countries.

Cuban and Venezuelan educationalists have agreed on the content of the programs and the method of recording classes for both the first to fourth grade course and the fifth to sixth grade course. Cuban teachers recorded six classes for use in any country, while their Venezuelan counterparts recorded the geography and history classes. The course taking students up to sixth grade uses the same technical materials (television, video tapes) as Mission Robinson, and facilitators guided by adult education teachers—all Venezuelan—to guarantee the educational direction. Cuba is advising a group of assessors and the classes are recorded, edited, and reproduced on the island.

Similarly, we are collaborating with Missions Ribas and Sucre, providing advisors and logistical support. From the 1960s onwards Cuba has been developing, in real life, the concept of the universalization of higher education and has created the conditions for all school leavers to have access to university studies, based on a national education system that extends throughout the island, and through an extensive scholarship network.

Within that concept a new response has emerged in recent years: the municipalization of higher education, which allows all school leavers access to university careers. This idea goes beyond the training of professionals to meet the demands of the economy. At the center of the municipalization of university is the cultural and educational advancement of individuals and, in the final analysis, is for the people. That unique Cuban experience has been placed at Venezuela's disposal, which has distinct realities in terms of its huge number of school leavers without access to higher education, and its particular labor requirements.

In relation to Mission Sucre and the Bolivarian University, our country has opened up its experience in the municipalization of higher education. Venezuela has been able to adapt it to its own circumstances and is giving it a lot of support. Reaching that point took us 40 years. Venezuela can attain it much sooner, thanks to the organizational precedent and the mass experience of recorded courses contributed by Missions Robinson I and II.

With Missions Robinson, Ribas and Sucre, Plan Simoncito (kindergarten), and the Bolivarian schools, Venezuela is placing itself in the vanguard of profound educational changes for the peoples of Latin America. It is a great source of joy for Cuba to humbly and efficiently accompany it in its magnificent liberationist Bolivarian project. As President Chávez understands it: the foremost power of the people is knowledge.

Bolívar asked that morality and enlightenment transform our peoples. José Martí expressed it another way: "To be educated is the only way to be free." From Cuba we see clearly that Venezuela is advancing like never before toward that only way of being free.

also available from ocean press

CUBAN REVOLUTION READER
A Documentary History of 45 Key Moments in the Cuban Revolution
Edited by Julio García Luis

From the euphoria of the early years of the revolution to its near collapse in the 1990s, the editor selects a broad range of material, providing a sweeping vision of revolutionary Cuba—its challenges, its defeats, its impact on the world.

ISBN 1-920888-05-5 *(Also available in Spanish 1-920888-08-X)*

JOSÉ MARTÍ READER
Writings on the Americas
Edited by Deborah Shnookal and Mirta Muñiz

An outstanding anthology of the writings, letters and poetry of one of the most important Latin American voices of the 19th century. Teacher, journalist, revolutionary and poet, José Martí interweaves the threads of Latin American culture and history, fervently condemning the brutality and corruption of the Spanish colonizers as well as the increasingly predatory ambitions of the United States in Latin America.

ISBN 1-875284-12-5

LATIN AMERICA
From Colonization to Globalization
Noam Chomsky in conversation with Heinz Dietrich

An indispensable book for those interested in Latin America and the politics and history of the region. As Latin America hovers on the brink of a major social and economic crisis, Noam Chomsky discusses some of the principal political events in recent years.

ISBN 1-876175-13-3

CHILE: THE OTHER SEPTEMBER 11
An Anthology of Reflections on the 1973 Coup in Chile
Edited by Pilar Aguilera and Ricardo Fredes

Contributions by Ariel Dorfman, Salvador Allende, Pablo Neruda, Víctor and Joan Jara, Beatriz Allende, Fidel Castro, and others.

ISBN 1-876175-50-8 *(Also available in Spanish 1-876175-72-9)*

also available from ocean press

DVD: CHÁVEZ, VENEZUELA AND THE NEW LATIN AMERICA
An interview with Hugo Chávez by Aleida Guevara

In February 2004, Aleida Guevara conducted an extended, exlusive interview with Hugo Chávez, president of Venezuela, exploring Venezuela's revolutionary terrain post-April 2002—when Chávez survived a coup attempt supported by the United States. Featuring a dramatic interview with Jorge García Carneiro, newly appointed head of the Venezuelan armed forces, and street interviews with Venezuelans involved in the country 's many social programs, this film affords a rare opportunity to glimpse through the blockade of information imposed by the United States and into a country rich with hope, dreams, and... oil.

NTSC DVD / 55 MINUTES / COLOR / NOT RATED
SPANISH WITH ENGLISH SUBTITLES
ORDER DIRECT FROM OCEAN PRESS

CAPITALISM IN CRISIS
Globalization and World Politics Today
Fidel Castro

Cuba's leader adds his voice to the growing international chorus against neoliberalism and globalization. Includes Fidel's 1999 speech in Venezuela soon after the election of Hugo Chávez as president.

ISBN 1-876175-18-4

GLOBAL JUSTICE
Liberation and Socialism
Ernesto Che Guevara

Is there an alternative to the neoliberal globalization ravaging our planet?
  Collected here are three of Guevara's classic works, presenting his revolutionary view of a different world in which human solidarity and understanding replace imperialist aggression and exploitation.

ISBN 1-876175-45-1 *(Also available in Spanish 1-876175-46-X)*

LATIN AMERICA
Awakening of a Continent
Ernesto Che Guevara

Here, for the first time in one volume, is a comprehensive overview of Che Guevara's unique perspective on the continent of Latin America, showing his cultural depth and rigorous intellect.

ISBN 1-920888-38-1 *(Also available in Spanish 1-876175-71-0)*

also available from ocean press

CUBA AND VENEZUELA
Germán Sánchez

Cuba and Venezuela is a comparative historical analysis of the Cuban Revolution and the process of change and revolution currently unfolding in Venezuela. Including interviews, articles, and essays on the similarities and differences between the two Caribbean nations in the fields of culture, commerce, diplomacy, and social development, the author uncovers the foundations of a strong relationship between these two nations.

ISBN 1-920888-39-X *(Also available in Spanish 1-920888-34-9)*

THE CUBAN REVOLUTION AND VENEZUELA
Pamphlet Series

Sánchez examines the early years of both revolutions, teasing out the differences and similarities in their early actions, their historical antecedents, and the nature and rate of change in both countries. He provides a profound analysis of the shared history between Cuba and Venezuela, from the independence wars against Spain to the many joint social, political, and cultural projects unfolding today.

ISBN 1-920888-41-1 *(Also available in Spanish 1-920888-43-8)*

CHÁVEZ
Venezuela and the New Latin America
Hugo Chávez, interviewed by Aleida Guevara

Is Venezuela the new Cuba? Elected by overwhelming popular mandate in 1998, Hugo Chávez is now one of Latin America's most outspoken political figures.

In this extraordinary interview with Aleida Guevara, Chávez expresses a fiercely nationalist vision for Venezuela and a commitment to a united Latin America.

ISBN 1-920888-00-4 *(Also available in Spanish 1-920888-22-5)*

oceanpress

e-mail info@oceanbooks.com.au
www.oceanbooks.com.au